YOUR KNOWLEDGE HAS VALUE

AF150771

- We will publish your bachelor's and master's thesis, essays and papers

- Your own eBook and book - sold worldwide in all relevant shops

- Earn money with each sale

Upload your text at www.GRIN.com
and publish for free

Christopher King

Aus der Reihe: e-fellows.net stipendiaten-wissen

e-fellows.net (Hrsg.)

Band 809

Review Essay: Poor Economics (Banerjee/Duflo)

GRIN Verlag

Bibliografische Information der Deutschen Nationalbibliothek:

Die Deutsche Bibliothek verzeichnet diese Publikation in der Deutschen National-
bibliografie; detaillierte bibliografische Daten sind im Internet über http://dnb.d-
nb.de/ abrufbar.

Dieses Werk sowie alle darin enthaltenen einzelnen Beiträge und Abbildungen
sind urheberrechtlich geschützt. Jede Verwertung, die nicht ausdrücklich vom
Urheberrechtsschutz zugelassen ist, bedarf der vorherigen Zustimmung des Verla-
ges. Das gilt insbesondere für Vervielfältigungen, Bearbeitungen, Übersetzungen,
Mikroverfilmungen, Auswertungen durch Datenbanken und für die Einspeicherung
und Verarbeitung in elektronische Systeme. Alle Rechte, auch die des auszugsweisen
Nachdrucks, der fotomechanischen Wiedergabe (einschließlich Mikrokopie) sowie
der Auswertung durch Datenbanken oder ähnliche Einrichtungen, vorbehalten.

Imprint:

Copyright © 2013 GRIN Verlag GmbH
Druck und Bindung: Books on Demand GmbH, Norderstedt Germany
ISBN: 978-3-656-51070-3

This book at GRIN:

http://www.grin.com/en/e-book/262778/review-essay-poor-economics-banerjee-
duflo

GRIN - Your knowledge has value

Der GRIN Verlag publiziert seit 1998 wissenschaftliche Arbeiten von Studenten, Hochschullehrern und anderen Akademikern als eBook und gedrucktes Buch. Die Verlagswebsite www.grin.com ist die ideale Plattform zur Veröffentlichung von Hausarbeiten, Abschlussarbeiten, wissenschaftlichen Aufsätzen, Dissertationen und Fachbüchern.

Visit us on the internet:

http://www.grin.com/

http://www.facebook.com/grincom

http://www.twitter.com/grin_com

Indiana University

College of Arts & Sciences

Department of Political Science

Spring 2013

POLS-Y343: Politics of International Development

Review Essay

Banerjee, Abhijit V.; Duflo, Esther (2011):

Poor Economics. A radical rethinking of the way to fight global poverty

Christopher King

International Exchange Student in the Undergraduate Program

Table of Content

"After all, we have spent billions of dollars on aid. [...] Has it done any good? And sadly, we don't know. And worst of all, we will never know." (Duflo 2010, 01:37)

1. Introduction

Poverty alleviation is a huge humanitarian challenge and also the supreme discipline of some economists. The effort to fight poverty had a mixed success so far and scholars claim different reasons for that outcome (cf. Besley 2012). In "Poor Economics", Abhijit Banerjee and Esther Duflo avoid the often polemic 'Sachs vs. Easterly' aid debate and promise a "radical rethinking of the way to fight global poverty": They make a convincing case about learning on the lives of the poor and the unique choices they have to face in their lives. Banerjee/Duflo understand how the poor perceive their conditions and come to the decision they make and are therefore able to craft better strategies and interventions that actually help the poor and do not produce unintended consequences. By doing that, they deliberately target the micro-level and leave out the level of politics or institutions, which is somewhat problematic, to search effective approaches in answers of the smaller questions.

This essay is structured in the following way: After an introduction to the analysis (2.) and an overview of Randomized Controlled Trials (RCTs), the main method of Banerjee/Duflo (2.1), the analysis will provide an assessment of key examples of the two scholars' research (2.2). Subsequently, an evaluation of limitations (2.3) and shortcomings (2.4) of the book will be conducted. By evaluating the approach and findings of "Poor Economics", the essay will be able to compare it with other scholarly works (3.). A conclusion (4.) will summarize the review and end with a personal take on what has been learned through studying the book.

2. Analysis

Banerjee/Duflo claim that most aid today is based on untested assumptions or even misperceptions of the lives and decisions of the poor. According to them, this can be drastically changed and the conditions of the poor understood through effective interventions that were tested on the ground. Their approach can be summarized in that they want to a) try to stay out of the mainstream aid debate between Sachs and Easterly, b) understand the life, situation, behavior and constraints of the poor and c) create and test innovative interventions.

2.1 Randomized Controlled Trials

The main method Banerjee/Duflo use is the scientific approach of field experiments with Randomized Controlled Trials (RCTs), in which interventions are tested through treatment and control groups that are chosen at random. So Banerjee/Duflo, therefore sometimes called 'randomistas', use experiments to find better, respectively more efficient ways to fight global poverty. Besley called RCTs "one of the most important innovations in economists' tool kits" (Besley 2012) and Banerjee/Duflo are the scholars who pushed this tool in their Poverty Action Lab (J-PAL) forward and increased its credibility in the scientific community.

Some readers may feel that RCTs are morally wrong to execute because first, the other half of a group loses potentially out and second, one shouldn't experiment with the lives of the poor (cf. Easterly 2009). But most of the time, there is only enough money to apply the intervention for a portion of the population anyway. Regarding the experimental concern, Banerjee/Duflo would argue that human rights review boards grant clearance for them. Other criticism focuses on the hype of RCTs and their increasingly preferred use over other methods of gaining knowledge of the poor (see Easterly 2009, Deaton 2010). Despite the critics, Banerjee/Duflo argue that "push[ing] on the right lever can make a huge difference" (Banerjee/Duflo 2012: x) and it is their goal to find these levers with RCTs.

2.2 Key examples

One strong side of "Poor Economics" is the rich fundus of interventions that were tested successful with RCTs but also examples of aid policies that clearly did not work. Banerjee/Duflo devote the first part of the book to the private lives of the poor and the second part to markets and institutional approaches. What overall stands out is the insight the reader can gain into the lives of the poor, about the challenges and decisions they face that are so extremely different to those that people in developed countries have to deal with.

A lot of the data and knowledge that was gathered in the book is based on careful observations and interviews of the lives of the poor. A series of views into their research will follow to show what their findings is about: Banerjee/Duflo expose how the poor spend their money wrongly in terms of health – on cure instead prevention, on private providers or traditional healers that are expensive and by demanding wrong cures (cf. ibid., 51ff.). Their explanations are sound and convincing as they single out a lack of information and trust (cf. ibid., 58f.), as well as time inconsistency problems with prevention (short-sightedness). Banerjee/Duflo call for making the right choices easier to take for the poor, in one example by providing chlorine dispensers at water wells. Their solution depicts their ideology: They are, in cases where they tested it successfully, pro incentives and try to find subsidies/nudges (cf. ibid., 63ff.) to help the poor in making the right choices. Examples for this include their bed net study, in which they found with RCTs that handing them out for free or highly subsidized makes sense as the total use actually decreased when charging for them or the immunization study, in which they found that it is after all cheaper to give out lentils to people as an incentive for immunizing their children than not incentivizing the immunization at all.

These kinds of findings can be very helpful for policymakers who are interested in crafting the most efficient interventions for their respective countries. For example, the cognition of deworming children to increase their school years proved to be very effective and was taken up likewise by governments, policymakers and NGOs. But some cases are more convincing than others, at one point Banerjee/Duflo state "that there is no smoking gun to prove that larger families are bad for children" (ibid., 110) and don't find quality-quantity relationships/trade-offs, although they argued earlier that parents indeed pick winners and losers (cf. ibid., 88f.) out of their children to advantage one over others.

Overall, the first part of the book is an easier reading and also more impressive because it presents workable solutions, while the second part gets more technical but no less interesting and delves into the topics of insurance and lending to the poor. Micro-credit for example is very complex and presented as not the silver bullet some claim it to be, although it has its justified standing as a tool of poverty alleviation in certain cases (cf. ibid., 171). Banerjee/Duflo challenge Muhammad Yunus, the creator of microfinance, who "describe[d] the poor as natural entrepreneurs" (ibid., 207), in saying that many of the businesses of the poor emerge, because the poor "buy a job" as they have no access to other ones. After all, the poor may have as many good or bad entrepreneurs as developed countries (cf. ibid., 225). Microfinance is not black and white and they make a good job in showing the assets and drawbacks of microfinance on how the poor save.

2.3 Limitations

As promising RCTs can be seen, they also have inherent limitations in their application. The preceding examples show that RCTs are limited to test, respectively prove smaller interventions on the micro-level. Ironically, as the poor spend their money on expensive cures instead of prevention, the micro-interventions of Banerjee/Duflo have been seen as "treat[ing] the symptoms of poverty rather than their causes" (Thirlwall 2012: 1556).

Greater policy changes on the institutional level can hardly be tested with RCTs. Banerjee/Duflo would respond to that, that they very deliberately tackle the smaller ones, because it is exactly their approach: Understanding the conditions and consequential choices for the poor, to craft in the second step efficient interventions on the micro-level to change the developmental policies and achieve improvements at the margin.

Nora Lustig raises two other concerns in asking why certain results occur or not ("black box" problem) and by wondering about transferability capacity ("external validity") of many interventions that have been proven as 'successful' by RCTs (cf. Lustig 2012: 140). It is indeed quite unclear how transferable the results from RCTs are from one context to the other (cf. Thirlwall 2012: 1555) – William Easterly calls that even the „single biggest concern" (Easterly 2009) about RCTs. Quiet surprisingly then[1], he reviewed the book pretty friendly and wrote that it "deserve[s] to be congratulated—and to be read" (Easterly 2011) for its insight into the lives of the poor. Banerjee/Duflo would presumably defend the "external validity" of the interventions claimed as successful by promoting more RCTs, especially in the new context it should be transferred to. This sounds like a lot of experiments but Duflo defends it by claiming that with RCTs "[…] you can take the guess-work out of policy making by knowing what works, what doesn't work and why?" (Duflo 2010, 05:32).

2.4 Political detachment

The fantastic research of Banerjee/Duflo is to be applauded, because it improves development policy interventions and makes money therefore much more wisely spent. But I also don't think it is sufficient, because their successes can be prevented or reversed through crises like civil wars in societies, where the West has little to no influence on. To put it simply: Educated and well-nourished children won't be better off in the end if their environment gets destroyed by politics and civil war. Good Governance may be equally important for poverty alleviation, but they deliberately avoid big institutional politics. The political detachment may be the only big "flaw" of the book that justifies major criticism: Banerjee/Duflo rarely talk about the political level or institutions and by that, Besley argues, "neglect much of the bigger picture" (Besley 2012) as the greatest improvements in poverty alleviation so far have been made governments. To their defense, their policy improvements work not only for external interventions but also for government policies; however a counterfactual to their micro-focus is probably the case of China, where the state turned things around with wide approaches rather than micro-level solutions (cf. Besley 2012).

So one could criticize them for neglecting governmental institutions, as the conditions the

---

[1] or not, if you consider that Banerjee/Duflo criticize some contemporary aid policies as Easterly does so eagerly

poor live in are ultimately shaped by micro-interventions as well as by the macro-environment that is influenced by the respective institutions. Moreover, they (have to) limit themselves on countries where interventions are possible and the countries are actually interested in poverty alleviation. Banerjee addressed this and the criticism of the neglect of politics in an interview: "I don't think we were saying that politics is unimportant. You know, if you're in North Korea, we don't have anything to tell them and that's just how it is." (Aitkenhead 2012).

3. Placement in literature

Although they wish to distance themselves from the aid debate, Banerjee/Duflo refer to Sachs and Easterly throughout the book. They present them as the heated sides of the aid debate and arrange themselves as a pragmatic voice that wants to understand the poor through field experiments. They devote chapter 10 to their placement into the macroeconomic/political economic debates and call Easterly's anti-aid stance "superficially irresistible" (Banerjee/Duflo 2012: 247) but not feasible to achieve progress. They specifically go on at the "institutionalist view" that demands big answers and good politics first, and expects the right policies to potentially emerge out of it (cf. ibid., 236). In addition to that, they criticize the "melancholist view", represented by their MIT colleague Daron Acemoglu and James Robinson, who state in their book "Why Nations Fail" that good (inclusive) institutions are the key factor for success. Banerjee/Duflo want to remain more optimistic and count on significant change despite bad institutions. For Acemoglu/Robinson, institutions always tops everything else and can only be changed to the good through big changes like revolutions, but Banerjee/Duflo call for a "quiet revolution" (ibid., 265) and also claim that politics, like policies, "can (and must) be improved at the margin" (ibid., 253).

So "Poor Economics" is not about why some countries are poor and others not, but about improving the development policies in countries where it is possible/wanted by the government as for example in India, Indonesia, Morocco or Kenya. This is an important point, as Sachs/Easterly focus on international aid, but most money spent on the poor is actually spent by the respective governments of the countries (cf. ibid., 5). Gaining knowledge through experiments can improve their policies and Banerjee/Duflo claim that interventions can have success even without fixing politics first.

4. Conclusion

Banerjee/Duflo promised to the beginning of "Poor Economics": "This book will not tell you whether aid is good or bad, but it will say whether particular instances of aid did some good or not." (ibid., 4). A main concern of Banerjee/Duflo is to be confident in positively answering the introductory question of the essay in the future. They focus on making development policy smarter, and I'm positive that they accomplished this in more than 10 years of their research on RCTs at and beyond J-PAL. Maybe if their knowledge had been produced earlier and they were as famous as they are now, some scholars would not need to be so negative against aid interventions. Although some limitations are present in the book, namely the diminished role of politics, they do not make "Poor Economics" a poor book.

Personally, the book gave me great insight into the lives of the poor in the world and the second part is an excellent introduction into microfinance. Moreover, the book teaches to get to the bottom of things to understand it, to question some ways of contemporary aid and to not take correlation as sufficient for causality in research. For these reasons alone it is an essential read for an undergraduate interested in development economics and poverty alleviation.

5. Bibliography

Aitkenhead, Decca (2012): Abhijit Banerjee: 'The poor, probably rightly, see that their chances of getting somewhere different are minimal'. In: *The Guardian*. London. Available online at http://www.guardian.co.uk/books/2012/apr/22/abhijit-banerjee-poor-chances-minimal, checked on 04/08/2013.

Banerjee, Abhijit V.; Duflo, Esther (2012, c2011): Poor economics. A radical rethinking of the way to fight global poverty. Pbk.ed. New York: PublicAffairs.

Besley, Timothy (2012): Poor Choices. Poverty From the Ground Level. Foreign Affairs. Available online at http://www.foreignaffairs.com/articles/136936/timothy-besley/poor-choices, checked on 04/08/2013.

Deaton, Angus (2010): Instruments, Randomization, and Learning about Development. In *Journal of Economic Literature* 48 (2), pp. 424–455.

Duflo, Esther (2010): Social experiments to fight poverty. TED. Long Beach, CA, 2010. Available online at http://www.ted.com/talks/esther_duflo_social_experiments_to_fight_poverty.html, checked on 04/08/2013.

Easterly, William (2009): Development Experiments: Ethical? Feasible? Useful? Available online at http://aidwatchers.com/2009/07/development-experiments-ethical-feasible useful/, checked on 04/08/2013.

Easterly, William (2011): Measuring How and Why Aid Works—or Doesn't. In: *The Wall Street Journal*. Available online at http://online.wsj.com/article/SB10001424052748703956904576287262026843944.html, checked on 04/08/2013.

Lustig, Nora (2012): Poor Economics: A Radical Rethinking of the Way to Fight Global Poverty. In *Feminist Economics* 19 (1), pp. 137–141.

Thirlwall, A.P (2012): Poor Economics: A Radical Rethink of the Way to Fight Global Poverty – A Review Article. In *Journal of Development Studies* 48 (10), pp. 1554 1557.